Making a Motorway

by
James Dallaway
photographs by
Jane Miller

Wayland

Words printed in **bold** in the main text are
explained in the glossary on page 31.

Cover: A scraper, for scraping up soil, is loaded onto a low-
loader ready to be taken somewhere else.

Opposite: A tyre for a scraper costs as much as a family car.

Editors: James Kerr, Heather Ancient
Designer: Malcolm Walker

First published in 1992 by
Wayland (Publishers) Limited
61 Western Road, Hove
East Sussex BN3 1JD, England

British Library Cataloguing in Publication Data
Dallaway, James
    Making a motorway
    I. Title
    625.7

ISBN 0-7502-0476-1

Typeset in England by Kudos Editorial and Design Services
Printed in Italy by G.Canale & C.S.p.A.
Bound in France by A.G.M.

Preparation for building a motorway starts long before the actual **construction** work begins.

First of all, government planners suggest that a motorway is needed between two places, maybe passing other towns on the way. The engineers are asked to see whether a motorway can actually be built along the suggested route. Is the route very hilly? Are there lots of things in the way, like buildings, rivers and railways? These questions will be answered by the **surveyors** (below). Are there areas where people will object strongly to the building of a motorway because it could spoil the countryside? Generally speaking all these problems can be dealt with but sometimes it may cost a lot to do so and the government may decide the cost will outweigh the advantages of the motorway.

Very often public enquiries are held after the proposed route of the motorway is published. Anyone who feels the motorway

should not be built, or that the route should be altered, can go along and have their say. The inspector who holds the enquiry will listen to what everyone has to say and will eventually make a report to the government suggesting what should be done. The inspector may say the route of the motorway should be moved somewhere else, or that special measures, like building **embankments**, should be taken to cut down noise.

Whenever a motorway is planned, people will have different opinions as to whether it's a good idea or not. Often people in nearby towns are pleased because it may take away lorry traffic from their High Street. It can also make it easier and quicker for them to get to other places. On the other hand, people who live in the country close to where the motorway will pass are usually very unhappy. The building of the motorway can be messy, noisy and cause hold-ups on local roads. Once the motorway is built the roar of cars and lorries will destroy their peaceful environment.

Sometimes people who are against the motorway being built

form powerful opposition groups. They will organize marches, and they can delay the building of the motorway for a very long time.

If the plans are approved and the opposition overcome, the work of building the motorway can begin. A **contractor** is appointed to carry out the work. The contractor usually works under tight supervision of the engineer who has designed the road.

Digging, or excavating, is usually the first operation in building a motorway, but before they start the drivers of the machines have to know where to dig. Engineers have to 'set out' the ground first. The pegs the engineer and his helper are putting in the ground mark the edge of the route and also show the excavator driver how deep to dig.

The people who operate the excavators are called digger drivers. Here an engineer is telling the driver what he wants him to do. In the background you can see some red and white posts with sloping rails fixed to them. These are called batter rails and show the digger driver where to dig and what angle the side of the cut must be. If the sides are too shallow the cut will take up too much land; if they are too steep they may collapse.

Before the main digging begins the topsoil is stripped. This means that the first layer of loose soil, which is suitable for growing plants, is carefully scraped up and stored so that it can be used again. The picture shows the ground after the topsoil strip is finished and the **subsoil** underneath is exposed.

Sometimes motorways have to be built across ground that is not suitable to carry the road and the heavy traffic that will use it. When the topsoil on this site was removed it exposed an old gravel pit filled with rubbish. The rubbish contains soft materials which will sink under the weight of the motorway and its traffic. The motorway must have a firm base, so all the rubbish has to be dug out and cleared away.

Sometimes the rubbish that was buried in these pits many years ago may include substances that rot and produce a gas called methane which can cause explosions. This gas, and other poisonous substances such as asbestos and chemicals that may be in the rubbish, can be dangerous to the workers building the motorway.
The engineer is testing to see whether there is any gas still in the ground.

These dump trucks are being filled by the red and white machine called a backactor, which excavates the site. The dump trucks are called **articulated** because they are able to bend in the middle.

These dump trucks have just started to refill the hole with suitable material for the motorway base. This is usually soil mixed with plenty of sand and gravel which will make a firm base and drain well. It has to be spread out in layers which are **compacted** with rollers. This ensures that the base will not sink under the motorway when it is in use.

Motorways are designed, using computers, to have what is called a muck balance. This means that the soil removed from where the motorway passes through hilly ground should be used in filling up the parts where the motorway is higher than the existing ground. The aim is to have no soil left over, nor to have to bring extra soil from elsewhere as this can be very expensive. This big dump truck is taking soil from a high part along a **haul road** to fill up a low part.

As far as is possible, motorways are routed to avoid existing buildings, especially people's homes. Sometimes there is no alternative and buildings have to be knocked down. This machine is using a big tool called a breaker to demolish an old factory. Lying in the front of the picture is the bucket for scooping up the rubble. This can be fixed on the machine in place of the breaker.

Sometimes it is not possible to dig up soil from one place and put it down in another immediately. It has to be stored for a while in spoil heaps. Here a large machine called a face shovel has dug a bucketful out of the spoil heap and is loading it into a dumper so it can be taken to a place which needs filling.

This is quite an old machine called a dragline. It is used for digging wide and deep cuts below ground level. The driver can throw out the bucket a long way, rather like casting out a fishing line. The bucket is then dragged back towards the machine and collects soil on the way.

Bulldozers are used for all sorts of work, like pulling scrapers and rollers, but this is the job that they were really designed for. This one is spreading out the chalk that the upper levels of the motorway will be laid on into even layers which will later be compacted by the rollers.

There are many smaller jobs to be done when a motorway is being built, and these are two of the machines that help out. The machine with tracks can be fitted with all sorts of different tools like excavating buckets and concrete breakers. This one has a specially-shaped tool for breaking up old concrete roads or hard rock. The wheeled machine has a shovel on the front and an excavating bucket at the back for digging trenches.

This tractor is shovelling some chalk over a concrete drainage pipe to protect it. The chalk spreads the load from the motorway and traffic, and so stops the pipe from cracking under the weight above it. This particular machine is a JCB, named after the initials of the man who designed it. However, nowadays people tend to call all tractor shovels like this JCBs, in the same way people tend to call all vacuum cleaners Hoovers.

There are always many drains to be dug when a motorway is being built. The water that falls on a motorway when it rains has to be channelled away, otherwise the roadway might become flooded. This trench is about as deep as a two-storey house. The sides have been propped up by a frame so they don't cave in on top of anyone working in it. The excavator is being used as a crane to lower in a length of drainpipe.

This machine is called a grader. The grader's blade can be moved in all sorts of directions to alter its height, angle and position. It is used to smooth down the surface, called the formation, on which the upper layers of the motorway will be laid. The formation can either be the existing ground or soil that has been placed there to bring the ground up to the required level.

After the formation is graded it has to be compacted to make it as firm as possible for the upper layers to be laid down. Here a big vibrating roller is being towed by a bulldozer. The roller is made to vibrate by the motor mounted on it. The vibration helps the roller compact the formation more than the roller would be able to using just its own weight. If you stand close to one of these machines you can feel the ground shake. After compaction the engineers will test the formation to see whether it is firm enough to carry the road surface.

Motorways are not just roads laid on the ground. Many bridges may have to be built. This picture shows part of a very complicated **intersection**, where two motorways cross each other. Here there is also a railway crossing the motorway. The railway tunnel and the bridge over it are built using reinforced concrete. The bridge with the crane on it is built mainly of steel sitting on concrete columns.

This is the beginning of a wall which will eventually support a bridge. The cage-like bars on the left-hand side are made of steel. On the right large moulds called formwork have been placed either side of the steel cage and concrete is being poured in. In this picture the concrete is being pumped in through a tube by the machine that looks like a crane. When the concrete sets, the formwork is removed, leaving a reinforced concrete wall which is strengthened by the steel bars inside it.

These men are placing concrete for a bridge. Look at the **falsework** underneath them. This holds up the bridge while it is being built. When all the concrete has been poured in and has hardened, the falsework will be removed and the bridge will stand up by itself. The man in the white helmet is using a vibrator which helps push the concrete into all the places it should be and also brings air bubbles to the surface. This is important because air bubbles trapped in the concrete make weak spots.

This bridge is being built in a different way. The large beams you see in the picture have been made in a factory and brought to the site by road. Some of them have been put in position already and the cranes are just going to lift another from the transporter. Building a bridge in this way avoids the need for the falsework you saw in the last picture. Using two cranes together to lift loads like this is quite complicated because the two drivers have to work together as a team. When the beams are all in place, wet concrete will be put between them to join them together.

Some of the structures on motorways, particularly the bigger bridges, have to have special **foundations**. The soil near ground level may not be strong enough to prevent the bridge supports from sinking. **Piles** are used to carry the weight of the bridge down to firmer soil or rock below. This machine, called an auger rig, is just starting to bore a hole in the ground down to the stronger rock below. When the auger rig has bored out all the soil the hole will be filled with concrete and steel reinforcement which together form the pile.

There are all sorts of piles. Here these big steel tubes are being driven into the ground to support a bridge. The dirty yellow machine in the middle of the picture is a big diesel-driven hammer which has nearly finished driving the first pile in. It is very noisy and the workers are wearing earmuffs to protect their hearing. Half this road has been closed and the traffic is controlled by temporary traffic lights while the work is done.

While the motorway is being built traffic on roads crossing the motorway site has to be kept moving. The engineers have to work out careful plans to manage the traffic so that there is as little disruption as possible. Here a big temporary bridge has been put up over the new motorway until a new bridge is built. This kind of temporary bridge is very easy to put up and take down. It is called a Bailey bridge after the man who invented it for use by soldiers in wartime.

Road traffic is not the only thing that has to be provided for when a motorway is being built. This farm has been cut in half by the road. A new bridge, called an accommodation bridge, is being built so that the farmer can take the cows from one side to the other. Until it is finished the cows have to cross over the new motorway site.

This is the beginning of laying the road on the formation. This grader is smoothing out dry-lean concrete to form the lowest layer of the road which is called the sub-base. Dry-lean concrete is mainly gravel and sand with just enough cement and water to firm it. Sometimes crushed rock is used, without any cement. It will be rolled and compacted next.

Motorways are built in different ways depending on what the ground underneath is like, what materials are available in the area, and the latest ideas on improvements in road building and ways of cutting costs. This motorway has a concrete base without any steel reinforcement in it. The picture shows the front of the concreting train which runs on rails at either side. This section roughly levels the concrete and vibrates it which makes it very solid and shakes air bubbles to the surface. The next section of the concreting train smooths the surface of the concrete.

This picture shows the other end of the concreting train with the concrete being finished off ready to have the final surface laid on it. Some roads have concrete surfaces but these are less popular nowadays because it is difficult to make them as smooth to ride on as those with **asphalt** surfaces. The concrete has to be protected carefully after it has been laid and covered to stop it drying too quickly and cracking.

Now the asphalt surface of the motorway is put down. This machine is called a paver. The truck tips crushed rock coated with bitumen into the front end of the paver which slowly moves along laying it evenly on the concrete layer. This will make the surface that the traffic uses. It's a bit like concrete, made with crushed rock, but instead of using cement to firm it, it is mixed with bitumen which we get from oil. The bitumen has to be used hot so that it can be spread and rolled. It sets as it cools but never gets as stiff as concrete. This makes a better road surface because it is smooth and **flexible** and is also easier to repair than concrete. It is usually called black-top.

After the paver come the rollers. The nearest one is the type that vibrates to press the surface down more firmly. The one behind is like those you see working on ordinary roads. The engineer is checking how well the roller has done its job with a nuclear densiometer. This measures how well the roller has compacted the black-top.

There are still quite a few finishing touches needed. This machine is cutting holes in the road surface for cat's-eyes to be set into. In the lower picture the worker has set a cat's-eye in the road and is pouring hot **pitch** around it. This will set and hold the cat's-eye in place. Cat's-eyes in the road reflect cars' headlights and mark the edges of the motorway lanes.

Now the crash barriers have to be fixed. These workers are driving in the supporting posts with a hammer on the wheeled trolley. It is a noisy job so they wear earmuffs. Crash barriers will be fixed on to the support posts.

These cranes are lifting up one of the sign **gantries**. These go over the motorway lanes and support signs that show directions and give information about traffic conditions and special speed limits.

At last the motorway is finished. There is usually a special opening ceremony and all sorts of important people, who have usually had very little to do with building the motorway, are invited. Speeches are made. Maybe the minister of transport will cut the ribbon stretched across the road and then be driven along it to inspect the work of the engineers and contractors. On this occasion it looks as though an old open Rolls Royce has been brought along especially for the minister's journey.

Motorways do not last for ever. The large numbers of vehicles and the weight of the traffic they carry means that the surfaces eventually have to be repaired or even rebuilt. This machine, called a scarifier, heats up the black-top that needs repairing in order to soften it, then scrapes it up and dumps it into the lorry behind. The old black-top is taken away to an asphalt **plant**, where it is heated and passed through a mixer. This recycled black-top will be used to build other roads and motorways.

Glossary

Articulated In two separate sections.

Asphalt A mixture of bitumen and gravel used for road surfacing.

Compacted Packed closely together.

Construction Building.

Contractor A person or firm that agrees to do a job or supply materials for a fee.

Embankments Ridges of earth or stone which carry or run alongside a road or railway.

Falsework A framework supporting something which is being built.

Flexible Able to bend.

Foundations A construction below the ground that supports a building, wall or road.

Gantries Frameworks which hold things up, such as signs.

Haul road A road used by vehicles carrying heavy loads.

Intersection A place where roads cross each other.

Piles Long columns of timber, steel or concrete which are driven into the ground to act as foundations.

Pitch A dark, sticky substance that is like tar.

Plant A factory or works.

Subsoil The layer of soil underneath the topsoil.

Surveyors People who measure and inspect pieces of land that are being built on.

Further reading

Road by Philip Steele (Eagle, 1991)
Roads by Kate Petty (A & C Black, 1991)
Road Travel by Tim Wood (Wayland, 1992)
Trucks by Ian Graham (Franklin Watts, 1990)

Index

Picture Acknowledgements

All pictures by Jane Miller except
page 4 Chapel Studios, page 5 Environmental Picture Library.